DISCOVER MY WORLD

Mountain

Written by Ron Hirschi
Illustrated by Barbara Bash

A BANTAM LITTLE ROOSTER BOOK
NEW YORK · TORONTO · LONDON · SYDNEY · AUCKLAND

MOUNTAIN

A Bantam Little Rooster Book / September 1992

Little Rooster is a trademark of Bantam Books, a division of Bantam Doubleday Dell
Publishing Group, Inc.

Library of Congress Cataloging-in-Publication Data

Hirschi, Ron.
  Mountain / by Ron Hirschi : illustrated by Barbara Bash.
    p. cm.—(Discover my world)
  "A Bantam little rooster book."
  Summary: Text and illustrations explore the variety of animal life
found on a mountain.
    ISBN 0-553-07998-0.—ISBN 0-553-35495-7 (pbk.)
    1. Alpine fauna—Juvenile literature.   [1. Alpine animals.]
I. Bash, Barbara, ill.   II. Title.   III. Series: Hirschi, Ron.
Discover my world.
QL113.H56   1992
599.0909'43—dc20   91-14368
                                                       CIP
                                                       AC

Published simultaneously in the United States and Canada

Bantam Books are published by Bantam Books, a division of Bantam Doubleday Dell
Publishing Group, Inc. Its trademark, consisting of the words "Bantam Books" and the
portrayal of a rooster, is Registered in U.S. Patent and Trademark Office and in other
countries. Marca Registrada. Bantam Books, 666 Fifth Avenue, New York, New York,
10103.

PRINTED IN HONG KONG

0 9 8 7 6 5 4 3 2 1

For William, Elizabeth, and Sophie
    —R.H.

For Michele—and her good eyes
    —B.B.

Hidden deep beneath
the winter snow,
mountain flowers
begin to grow.
Who will wake
when lilies bloom?
Who will appear
when spring is finally here?

Who are we,
twins born in a snug, warm den?

Who runs away
from the playful bears,
then stops, listens,
and stares?

Whose whiskers and tiny nose
sniff the heather trail
where bees buzz,
where beetles fly?

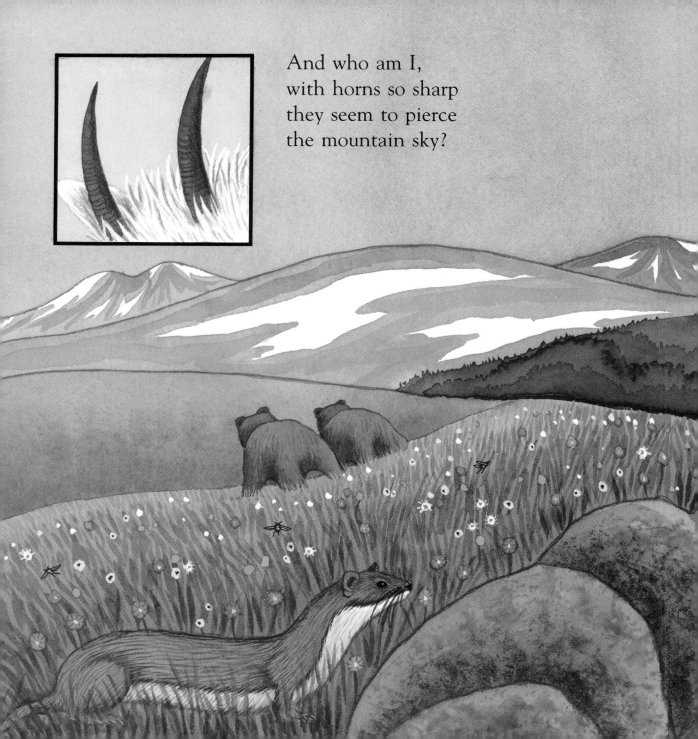

And who am I,
with horns so sharp
they seem to pierce
the mountain sky?

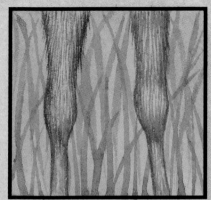

My knees wobble
when I walk my first steps
following my mother and brother.
Can you guess my name?

Who am I,
searching for a safe place
to raise my family?

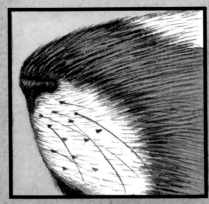

Wheeee! Wheeee! Wheeee!
Who am I,
the mountain whistler,
warning my neighbors
when danger is near?

Who walks silently
past the marmot's rock
on soft and padded paws?

And who pops out,
then back in its hole—
quickly—
when the lynx sneaks near?

Can the ground squirrel
see my shadow?
Can you see me
soaring high
like a soft, golden cloud?

Who hops into
someone's lunch?

And who followed
the gray jay,
holding out a gentle hand?
Could it be you?
Or could it be me?

 When glacier lilies bloom, they poke their stems through thin layers of melting snow, painting the meadows yellow. Their leaves are eaten by marmots, elk, snowshoe hare, and other animals.

 Baby bears are born in a winter den beneath the ground. They crawl out with their mothers as the snowfields melt in spring. Then they nurse and learn to eat grass, seeds, and animals, too.

 The snowshoe hare puts on one coat for winter and another one for spring, blending with the snow or with the meadow grasses. Never completely hidden, snowshoe hares are prey of the bobcat, coyote, golden eagle, and other predators.

 Weasels also change their coats to match the seasons and use their camouflage coloring and fierce determination to catch mice and other mountain animals, including many twice their size.

ountain Discoveries

 Mountain goats live only in the American West. Their feet are specially adapted to cling to slippery surfaces, helping them to climb the steepest slopes. But rocky cliffs can be dangerous and some goats do fall from the mountains.

 A baby elk, like a deer fawn, is spotted when very young. But the elk's spots cannot help it hide from predators when it must walk with its mother to a new feeding place. It must especially beware of grizzly bears.

 Wolves have vanished from most of the United States. Strong family ties, group recognition, and vocal or visual communication bind wolves together where they have survived.

 A marmot's whistle is as much a part of the mountain wilderness as the loon's call in our northern lakes. This burrowing mammal hibernates, emerging in spring to eat mountain wildflowers and bask in the sun.

 A lynx's padded feet are oversized like snowshoes, to help keep it from falling through crusts of snow. Excellent tree climbers, lynx will sit in branches, then jump on their prey.

 Ground squirrels duck down into their burrows to avoid predators. They also curl up in their burrows during their long summer sleep. This estivation is somewhat like the winter hibernation of other animals.

 Golden eagles nest in mountain cliffs and in treetops. They hunt, using their keen eyesight to spot their prey. Then the eagles swoop from high in the sky to catch rabbits, ground squirrels, or other small animals.

 Gray jays are curious and will sneak into your lunch basket or backpack to snack on peanuts. One of the most approachable animals, they offer you the chance to watch as they sit nearby or hop onto your hand.